BIBLE SAYS

The Future Anti-Christ

What the Bible Says:

The Future Antichrist

Published by: Armor Books
P. O. Box 1050
Lawrenceville, GA 30045
Web Site: http://www.armorbooks.com
All rights reserved.

This is a derivative writing taken from the collective works of the late Finis Jennings Dake, and used by permission of the copyright holders. Unless otherwise noted, all Scripture quotations are from the Holy Bible, King James Version

ISBN: 1-55829-077-X (paperback)

01 02 03 04 05   87654321

CONTENTS

PREFACE

For many Christians, the Bible is a book of mystery, full of hidden meaning only to be understood by pastors and seminarians who have devoted lifetimes to uncovering the truths found within its pages. Latin was the language of the Bible for centuries, and many still approach the Scriptures as if they were written in a foreign tongue. A few stories are learned in Sunday School, a handful of popular verses memorized, but many Christians fear to turn the pages of their Bibles into unfamiliar territory.

But there is no reason to be afraid. The Bible is the easiest book in the world to understand. You don't need to be a pastor or have a seminary degree. God designed the Bible to be understood by you and me, and the truths He intended for us to learn are easily found within its pages.

The *"What the Bible Says"* booklets are designed to illustrate simple biblical truths on topics that many consider to be particularly difficult to grasp. This book strives to let the Bible speak for itself, and therefore, a comprehensive list of scripture references for each of the topics discussed will be presented. Although it's not necessary to look up each and every reference in order to understand what the Bible is saying on a particular topic, we'll focus on the primary references, and provide a thorough list of supporting scriptures for you to study on your own.

HOW TO UNDERSTAND THE BIBLE

Here's the most important rule to follow when studying the Bible: You must take the Bible literally wherever it is at all possible. Obviously, there are times when the language of the Bible cannot be taken literally, and then we know it is to be understood figuratively. When this is the case, it is our job to find the literal truth conveyed by the figurative language, just as if it were expressed in literal language without the use of figures. For more on this topic, see Appendix One, "Biblical Studies."

FIGURATIVE LANGUAGE OF THE BIBLE

The Bible contains some figurative language. A lot of confusion is caused when literal passages of scripture are mistakenly understood figuratively, and the same holds true for scripture that is interpreted as literal, when it is obviously figurative in nature. So, what is figurative language in the Bible? How can we recognize it when we find it? Simply put, figurative language, or a "figure of speech" occurs when we use words in a different sense from that which is ordinarily given them. Figures of speech are used to give emphasis and to add attraction and variety to human expression. It is important to note that they are never used for the purpose of doing away with literal truth. Instead, figures of speech set forth

Simply put, figurative language, or a "figure of speech" occurs when we use words in a different sense from that which is ordinarily given them. Figures of speech are used to give emphasis and to add attraction and variety to human expression.

literal truth in another form than that in which it could be literally expressed. What we're looking for is the literal truth found in the figurative language. Above all, we must not permit figures of speech to do away with the intended truth. If we fail to understand the literal truth expressed by the figure of speech, then it has failed in its purpose.

Now that we understand figures of speech, how can we tell whether a particular statment is intended to be understood literally or figuratively? It's easy! There's a fundamental rule to keep in mind when determining whether the language is literal or figurative: Every statement in the Bible is to be understood literally, when at all possible, and where it is clear that it is literal; otherwise, it is figurative. In other words, what cannot be literal must be figurative. The subject matter itself will always make this clear.

There are two kinds of figures of speech we find in the Bible: first, there are those involving only a word, as in Gal. 2:9 where Peter, James, and John are called "pillars" of the Church; second, there are those involving a thought expressed in several words or sentences, such as the parable, allegory, symbol, type, riddle, fable, and enigma.

GOD'S PROMISES ARE ESPECIALLY SIMPLE

We've stated that many people think the Bible is hard to understand. In particular, this belief is held by many concerning the prophecies, the proverbs, and some figures of speech. However, these seemingly difficult parts of the Bible are no more difficult to understand than the sections of the Bible that deal with history, or those that many consider to be "simple." Prophecy is nothing more than history written beforehand and should be understood in this light. All riddles, allegories, types, symbols, and figures of speech are either explained in Scripture, or are clear in themselves as to their true meaning.

When it comes to the promises of God, there shouldn't be any misunderstanding about what they say or mean. Every promise of God is a simple statement of obligation to men that God will give them certain benefits when they meet certain conditions. All the promises of God are conditional, as can be seen in the Scriptures themselves. If you want to receive the promised benefits, you must accept the promise for what it says and meet the conditions required. You can then depend upon the fulfillment of God's promise *in this life*. Since God cannot lie, man is assured that what God has promised He is abundantly able to perform. None of God's promises need further interpretation. All that we must do is act upon what the Bible says and believe that God's promise will be fulfilled in our lives. Do not attach any other conditions to God's promises than what is plainly written. When the conditions are met the blessings will be realized. As the Apostle Paul writes in 2 Cor. 1:20, "For *all* the promises of God in Him are yea, and in Him Amen, unto the glory of God by us."

Chapter One

THE FUTURE ANTICHRIST

The Beast Out of the Sea

And I stood upon the sand of the sea, and saw a beast rise up out of the sea, having seven heads and ten horns, and upon his horns ten crowns, and upon his heads the name of blasphemy. And the beast which I saw was like unto a leopard, and his feet were as the feet of a bear, and his mouth as the mouth of a lion: and the dragon gave him his power, and his seat, and great authority. And I saw one of his heads as it were wounded to death; and his deadly wound was healed: and all the world wondered after the beast. And they worshipped the dragon which gave power unto the beast: and they worshipped

11

the beast, saying, Who is like unto the beast? who is able to make war with him? And there was given unto him a mouth speaking great things and blasphemies; and power was given unto him to continue forty and two months. And he opened his mouth in blasphemy against God, to blaspheme his name, and his tabernacle, and them that dwell in heaven. And it was given unto him to make war with the saints, and to overcome them: and power was given him over all kindreds, and tongues, and nations. And all that dwell upon the earth shall worship him, whose names are not written in the book of life of the Lamb slain from the foundation of the world. If any man have an ear, let him hear. He that leadeth into captivity shall go into captivity: he that killeth with the sword must be killed with the sword. Here is the patience and the faith of the saints. Here is wisdom. Let him that hath understanding count the number of the beast: for it is the number of a man; and his number is Six hundred threescore and six (Rev. 13:1-10, 18)

The "beast" in Revelation refers to the rise of a kingdom and, more particularly, to the Antichrist, the earthly head of the kingdom. It also symbolizes a supernatural spirit out of the Abyss, as we shall later see. Beasts in Scripture symbolize both kingdoms and kings (Dan. 2: 38-39; 7:2-7 with 7:17, 23), as well as supernatural powers which control the kingdoms. This passage is certainly not the only scripture referring to the Antichrist, but it is perhaps the most comprehensive, providing a wealth of detail

> The "beast" in Revelation refers to the rise of a kingdom and, more particularly, to the Antichrist, the earthly head of the kingdom. It also symbolizes a supernatural spirit out of the Abyss. Beasts in Scripture symbolize kingdoms and kings, as well as supernatural powers which control the kingdoms.

about the person of the Antichrist, as well as his rise to power. Let's take a look at what this passage has to tell us about this man.

Who is the Antichrist?

At the present time, this question can't be answered. Actually, the question is unanswerable and will remain so until the Antichrist personally makes a covenant with Israel for seven years (we'll take a look at this later—it's recorded in Dan. 9:27). Many in the past have speculated that it could be the pope, Stalin, Hitler, the United Nations, a variety of other tyrants from countries spanning the globe, numerous organizations, and powerful world figures. A great deal of harm has been done to the subject of prophecy by this kind of speculation, and it has caused many to turn their backs on the possibility of prophetic inspiration when they have seen the uninspired results of this kind of "guessing game." The following points prove that no man now prominent in world affairs could possibly be the Antichrist.

From Where Does the Antichrist Come?

We don't know who the Antichrist may be, but we do know from where he will come. The Scriptures are clear that the Antichrist *must* come from a particular geographic area. If we turn to the book of Daniel, we'll see how this is clearly illustrated.

> This image's head was of fine gold, his breast and his arms of silver, his belly and his thighs of brass, His legs of iron, his feet part of iron and part of clay. Thou sawest till that a stone was cut out without hands, which smote the image upon his feet that were of iron and clay, and brake them to pieces. Then was the iron, the clay, the brass, the silver, and the gold, broken to pieces together, and became like the chaff of the summer threshingfloors; and the wind carried them away, that no place was found for them: and the stone that smote the image became a

great mountain, and filled the whole earth (Dan. 2:32-35)

The first was like a lion, and had eagle's wings: I beheld till the wings thereof were plucked, and it was lifted up from the earth, and made stand upon the feet as a man, and a man's heart was given to it. As concerning the rest of the beasts, they had their dominion taken away: yet their lives were prolonged for a season and time. These great beasts, which are four, are four kings, which shall arise out of the earth (Dan. 7:4, 12, 17)

In Daniel 2 and 7 we have two visions that cover the world powers from Daniel's day to the Second Coming of Christ. The "head of gold" on the image (Dan. 2:32, 35, 38) and the "lion" (Dan. 7:4, 12, 17) symbolize Babylon, Nebuchadnezzar's kingdom. The "breast and arms of silver" on the image (Dan. 2:32, 35, 39) and the "bear" (Dan. 7:5, 12, 17) symbolize Medo–Persia, which followed Babylon in the punishment of Israel (Dan. 2:39; 5:24-31;

16

6:1-28; 8:1-4, 20; 10:1-20; 11:1-3; 2 Chron. 36:22; Ezra 1:1-3). The "belly and thighs of brass" on the image (Dan. 2:39) and the "leopard" (Dan. 7:6, 12, 17) symbolize the old Grecian Empire of Alexander the Great that followed Medo–Persia in the times of the Gentiles (Dan. 2:39; 8:20-21; 11:1-4). The "legs of iron" on the image (Dan. 2:33-35, 40) and the nondescript "beast" (Dan. 7:7-8, 17-27) symbolize the old Roman Empire that followed the Grecian Empire and its four divisions in the persecution of Israel. The "feet and toes" of iron and clay on the image (Dan. 2: 33-35, 41-44) and "the ten horns" on the non-

The "feet and toes" of iron and clay on the image (Dan. 2: 33-35, 41-44) and "the ten horns" on the nondescript beast (Dan. 7:8, 20-24) symbolize ten kings who will head ten separate governments from ten separate capitals inside the old Roman Empire in the days of the Second Coming of Christ.

descript beast (Dan. 7:8, 20-24) symbolize ten kings who will head ten separate governments from ten separate capitals inside the old Roman Empire in the days of the Second Coming of Christ.

Some call these ten kingdoms the Revived Roman Empire, but to be technical, there is no such thing as the revival of the Roman Empire. This would require the old Roman territory to be formed into one empire again, to be ruled by one man from Rome—something the Bible doesn't teach. Instead, the Scriptures are clear that there will be ten kingdoms formed inside of this territory instead of one empire (Dan. 2:44; 7:23-24; Rev. 17:8-17). It would be best to call these ten kingdoms the "Revised Roman Empire" due to the fact that they will be formed inside the old Roman territory.

Daniel did not see a little toe growing out of the ten toes in Daniel 2, but in Daniel 7 he did see a "little horn" growing out of the ten horns, which plucked up three of the ten horns by the roots (Dan. 7:7-8). This is explained by Daniel:

> The fourth beast shall be the
> fourth kingdom upon the earth

[the old Roman Empire, which
followed Babylon, Medo–Persia,
and Greece from Daniel's day
on], which shall be diverse from
all kingdoms . . . the ten horns
out of this kingdom are ten kings
that shall arise: and another shall
rise after them; and he shall be
diverse from the first [the ten],
and he shall subdue three kings
[of the ten] (Dan. 7:23-24)

This will give the Antichrist power over
four of the ten kings. The other six of the ten
will agree to give their power to this "little
horn," and he will then form the eighth kingdom of Revelation 17:8-17.

It is clear that this "little horn" arises "after"
the ten kingdoms are formed, not "before,"
and that he does not have anything to do
with the rise of the ten kingdoms. He does
not come until "after" they are fully formed
and exist for a "short space" (Dan. 7:8; Rev.
17:9-11). The "little horn" as well as the "ten
horns" are all future events, for in Revelation
13:1-8; 17:9-17 it is clear that the ten kings

give their power and kingdom to the Beast for forty–two months, and together they will fight against Christ at Armageddon.

In Daniel 8 we have a vision of a ram and an he–goat. The ram symbolizes Medo–Persia, the same as the silver in the image of Daniel 2 and the bear of chapter 7. The he–goat symbolizes the Grecian Empire the same as the brass in the image of Daniel 2 and the leopard of the seventh chapter. The he–goat had a notable horn between its eyes, which was broken off, and in its place grew four horns and "out of one of them came forth the little horn." The interpretation of these things is given as follows:

> The ram which thou sawest having two horns are the [two] kings of Media and Persia. And the rough goat is the king [kingdom] of Grecia: and the great horn that is between his eyes is the first king [Alexander the Great who founded the old Grecian Empire]. Now that being broken [Alexander having died], where-

as four stood up for it [that is, four horns grew on the he–goat instead of the great horn], four kingdoms shall stand up out of the nation [the Grecian Empire shall be divided into four kingdoms], but not in his [Alexander's] power. And in the latter time of their kingdom, when the transgressors are come to the full, a king of fierce countenance, and understanding dark

The "little horn" as well as the "ten horns" are all future events, for it is clear that the ten kings give their power and kingdom to the beast for forty–two months, and together they will fight against Christ at Armageddon.

sentences, shall stand up [that is, the little horn shall come out of one of these four divisions of the ancient Grecian Empire in the last days of the existence of these four kingdoms] . . . He shall also stand up against the Prince of princes [Jesus Christ]; but he shall be broken without hand" by Christ at His second advent (Dan. 8:20-25, emphasis added)

These four divisions of the old Grecian Empire would be known today as Greece, Turkey, Syria and Egypt. Four of Alexander's generals divided his empire after his death. Cassander took Greece and Macedon, Lysimachus took Asia Minor or present Turkey and Thrace, Seleucus took Syria and Babylonia, and Ptolemy took Egypt. (This can be verified by anyone who will get an encyclopedia and see the map of the old Grecian Empire and its four divisions after the death of Alexander).

The purpose of Daniel 8 in relation to Daniel 7 is to narrow down the coming of the Antichrist geographically from the ten kingdoms of the future Revised Roman Empire to four of the ten kingdoms, and reveal that Antichrist will come from either Greece, Turkey, Syria or Egypt.

In Daniel 8:9 it is definitely stated that "the little horn" will come from one of the four horns, "out of one of them came forth a little horn, which waxed exceeding great, toward the south (Egypt), and toward the east (Babylonia), and toward the pleasant land (Palestine)." This verse is interpreted in verse 23 as "in the latter time of their kingdom (the existence of Greece, Turkey, Syria, and Egypt), when the transgressors are come to the full, a king of fierce countenance, and understanding dark sentences, shall stand up" and fight against "the prince of princes" at his Second Advent.

The purpose of Daniel 8 in relation to Daniel 7 is to narrow down the coming of the Antichrist geographically from the ten kingdoms of the future Revised Roman Empire to four of the ten kingdoms, and reveal that Antichrist will come from either Greece, Turkey, Syria or Egypt.

If we didn't have the vision of Daniel 8, we would have a much broader range of countries from which to choose. The Antichrist could then come from England, Holland, Belgium, France, Switzerland, Spain, Portugal, Italy, Austria, Hungary, Yugoslavia, Albania, or some other part of the old Roman Empire outside of the four divisions of the Grecian Empire. However, since the verses in Daniel 8 narrow the territory down from the ten kingdoms of the Roman Empire to the four divisions of the Grecian Empire, we know he must come from either Greece, Turkey, Syria, or Egypt.

If the Antichrist is coming from either Greece, Turkey, Syria, or Egypt, then it is obvious that he cannot come from Italy (it couldn't have been Mussolini), the Vatican (it's not the pope), England, America, Germany, Russia, or any other country outside the boundaries of the ancient Grecian Empire.

The Antichrist will come from one of these four divisions of the ancient Grecian Empire and will overthrow the other three, thus reviving the Grecian Empire, which will become the eighth or leopard kingdom of Rev. 13:1-18; 17:1-17.

The Antichrist, the King of the North

In Daniel 11 we have a vision of wars between two of the four divisions of the Grecian Empire, Syria, and Egypt, which were fought over a period of about 150 years ending with Antiochus Epiphanes who reigned about 165 B.C. Then the prophet skips over to the end time and pictures the last war between Syria and Egypt, with the result that Syria will finally overthrow Egypt. Egypt is called "the king of the south" and Syria "the king of the north" in this vision.

In Daniel 11:36–12: 13, the prophet definitely identifies the Antichrist as "the king of the north" (Syria) at "the time of the end." The purpose of the vision was to show "what shall befall thy people (Israel) in the latter days"

> *The purpose of this vision over Daniel 7 and 8 is to narrow down the coming of the Antichrist geographically from the ten kingdoms of Daniel 7, and from the four kingdoms of Daniel 8 to the one kingdom of Daniel 11.*

(Dan. 10:14). The purpose of this vision over Daniel 7 and 8 is to narrow down the coming of the Antichrist geographically from the ten kingdoms of chapter 7, and from the four kingdoms of Daniel 8 to the one kingdom of chapter 11—the Syrian division of the old Grecian Empire—thus teaching that the Antichrist will come from Syria at the end time.

If the whole vision of Daniel 11 concerns only Egypt and Syria showing the latter–day war between them with the result that Egypt will be finally overthrown by Syria, then it proves that he will come from Syria and not Egypt, Greece or Turkey, the other three divisions of the old Grecian Empire.

"The king of the north" is the same as the "little horn" of Daniel 7 and 8, "the prince that shall come" of Daniel 9:26-27, "the son of perdition" and "man of sin" of 2 Thessalonians 2:1-12, and "the beast" of Revelation 13 as proven by the following:

1. All do according to their will for the same length of time, Dan. 7:25; 8:24; 11:36; 2 Thess. 2:10-12; Rev. 13:5-7.
2. All will exalt themselves above every god, Dan. 7:25; 8:25; 11:36-37; 2 Thess. 2:4; Rev. 13:1-18.
3. All are conquerors in the same territory at the same time, Dan. 7:8, 20-24; 8:23-25; 11:40-45; Rev. 13:1-18.
4. All speak blasphemies against God at the same time, Dan. 7:8, 11, 20-25; 8:

23-25; 11:36; 2 Thess. 2:4; Rev. 13:5.

5. All prevail against the saints and Jews during the tribulation, Dan. 7:21-26; 8: 24; 11:40-41; 12:1, 7; Mt. 24:15-22; Rev. 13:1-18; 14:9-11; 15:1-4; 20:4-6.

6. All come out of the ten kingdoms of Revised Rome and get power over the ten kingdoms and reign over them until all of them are destroyed at Armageddon, Dan. 7:7-8, 23, 24; 8:9, 22-25; 11:40-45; Rev. 13:1-4; 17:9-17; 19:19-21.

7. All change the times and laws for a time, Dan. 7:11, 21-27; 8:22-25; 11:35-45; 12:7; 2 Thess. 2:1-13; Rev. 13:1-8.

8. All reign "until" the Second Coming of Christ, Dan. 2:44; 7:11-14, 18, 21-26; 8:23-25; 9:27; 11:36-45; 12:7-13; 2 Thess. 2:8-12; Rev. 17:9-17; 19:19-21.

9. All continue the same length of time, Dan. 7:21-26; 8:22-25; 9:27; 11:40-45; 12:7-13; 2 Thess. 2:8-13; Rev. 13:5; 17: 9-17; 19:19-21.

10. All will be alive when the God of Heaven comes to set up His kingdom,

Dan. 2:44; 7:11-14, 18-26; 8:22-25; 9:27; 11:40-45; 12:7-13; 2 Thess. 2:8-13; Rev. 17:14; 19:19-21; 20:1-10.

11. All cause the greatest tribulation that ever will be on earth, Dan. 7:21-27; 8:19, 24-25; 9:27; 12:1, 7; Mt. 24:15-22; 2 Thess. 2:1-12; Rev. 7:14; 13:1-18; 14:9-11; 15:2-4; 20:4-6; Jer. 30:3-7.

12. All will do away with the Jewish daily sacrifices in the future temple and cause the "abomination of desolation," Dan. 7:25; 8:11-14; 9:27; 11:35-45; 12:11; Mt. 24:15-22; 2 Thess. 2:4; Rev. 13:1-18.

13. All will reign in the Jewish temple in Jerusalem, Dan. 8:9-14; 9:27; 11:45; 12:7; 2 Thess. 2:4; Rev. 11:1-2; 13:1-18.

14. All will disregard the God of the fathers, Dan. 7:11, 19-25; 8:22-25; 9:27; 11:38-39; 2 Thess. 2:1-12; Jn. 5:43; Rev. 13:1-8.

15. All will honor the devil and get their power from him, Dan. 8:24; 11:35-45; 2 Thess. 2:9; Rev. 13:1-4.

16. All will come to the same end and be slain by Christ at the Second Advent and then be cast into the Lake of Fire, Dan. 2:44-45; 7:11, 21-26; 11:45; 2 Thess. 2:8-12; Rev. 19:19-21.

When Will He Come into Prominence in World Affairs?

This question is also clearly answered in Scripture:

(1) In Daniel 7:24, we have definite proof that Antichrist cannot be revealed and be prominent in world affairs, until after the ten kingdoms are formed inside the Roman Empire. According to this verse, the ten kingdoms must first be formed and exist for some time as the seventh kingdom, or Revised Rome. The Antichrist will arise and gain control over all the ten kingdoms in the first 3½ years of the Week. By the middle of the Week he will be seen as the beast of Revelation 13 coming up out of the sea of humanity already with the seven heads and ten horns, which he will have conquered

before the middle of the Week. His coming out of the sea in the middle of the Week will be simply the recognition of his power by the ten kingdoms and his acceptance of them from the ten kings and the dragon (Rev. 13:2-4; 17:12-17). This verse further teaches that, because of his rise out of the ten kingdoms, he is to come out of obscurity and that his rise to power will be quick. Daniel saw the "little horn" rising so suddenly among the ten that he was bewildered (Dan. 7:7-8, 19-24). Therefore, no man can determine who the Antichrist will be until after the ten kingdoms are formed.

(2) The Antichrist cannot be revealed until the rapture as proved in the following passage:

> And now ye know what withholdeth that he might be revealed in his time. For the mystery of iniquity doth already work: only he who now letteth will let, until he be taken out of the way. And then shall that Wicked be revealed, whom the Lord shall

consume with the spirit of his mouth, and shall destroy with the brightness of his coming (2 Thess. 2:6-8)

How Long is His Reign?

He will reign over one of the ten kingdoms of Revised Rome at the beginning of the Week and will obtain control over the whole ten kingdoms during the last 3½ years (Rev. 13:5; 7:25; 12:7). It is in these last 3½ years that he will exalt himself above every God and will be worshipped by many of his subjects (Rev. 13:14-18; Dan. 8:25; 11:36-45; 2 Thess. 2:4).

Where is He to Reign?

During part of the last 3½ years he will reign in Jerusalem "in the glorious holy mountain" where the temple will be rebuilt (Dan. 11:45). He will sit "in the temple of God, showing himself that he is God" (2 Thess. 2:4). This temple is where the "abomination of desolation" will be placed (Dan. 9: 27; 12:7-13; Mt. 24:15-22; Rev. 11:1-2; 13: 12-18). Babylon, and not Rome, will be his place of reign until then.

The fact that there will be ten separate kingdoms with ten separate capitals and ten separate kings in the first 3½ years shows that up to the middle of the Week the Antichrist does not have one capitol where he reigns over the ten kingdoms, for they will not yet be under his control. Rome will be just one of the ten capitals and her king will reign over the territory of Italy and her possessions and not over all of Revised Rome. It is only when Antichrist becomes head of the ten kingdoms by the middle of the Week that he will establish one central throne in Jerusalem for all the newly formed empire. Even then, the kings will continue to rule under him (Rev. 17:9-17).

The Power of the Antichrist

The power of the Antichrist will come from Satan, the spirit of the Abyss, and the ten kings. His power has already been predicted by God and it will be given him in due time. It is God who will permit Satan and his agents to give their power to the Beast and inspire him in his evil designs (Dan. 8:24; 2 Thess. 2:8-12; Rev. 13:1-2). It is God who will put it into the hearts of the ten kings to give him their power for the purpose of destroying Mystical Babylon (Rev. 17:12-17). It is the satanic prince out of the Abyss (Rev. 11: 7; 17:8) who will be the executive of Satan's power to the Beast and who will inspire and back the Antichrist in all his diabolical activities. Satan will give to the Antichrist the world–kingdoms he offered Christ. Antichrist will accept them; Christ did not. The Antichrist must fight to possess them even as Christ would have had to do and will yet have to do. Antichrist

> *It is God who will permit Satan and his agents to give their power to the Beast and inspire him in his evil designs. It is God who will put it into the hearts of the ten kings to give him their power for the purpose of destroying Mystical Babylon.*

will succeed in this world conquest by conquering the Revised Roman Empire by the middle of the Week and all the northern and eastern countries of Asia and Europe by the end of the Week. Also he will obtain the cooperation of many other nations through the ministry of the three unclean spirits, who will help him fight against the Jews and Christ at the Second Advent. After his defeat at Armageddon by Christ, the Antichrist will be cast into the Lake of Fire. The Kingdom of God will succeed his kingdom and extend throughout all the earth. The power of the beast may be summarized as follows:

1. To blaspheme God (Dan. 7:8, 11, 20, 25; 11:36; Rev. 13:5-6).
2. To overcome saints (Rev. 7:9-17; 14: 13; 15:2-4).
3. To overcome the Jews (Dan. 7:21; 12:7; Rev. 13:7, 15).
4. To conquer many nations (Dan. 7:8, 20-24; 11:36-45; Ezek. 38–39) and rule them as he wills (Rev. 13:7).
5. To destroy Mystery Babylon (Rev. 17: 12-17).

6. To overcome and kill the two witnesses (Rev. 11:7).
7. To change times and laws (Dan. 7:25).
8. To understand mysteries (Dan. 8:23).
9. To protect the Jews as long as he desires, and also to succeed in destroying them for a period (Dan. 9:27; 2 Thess. 2:4; Rev. 11:1-2).
10. To work signs and wonders (Dan. 8:24; 2 Thess. 2:8-12; Rev. 13:1-18; 19:20).
11. To cause craft to prosper (Dan. 8:25).
12. To control money and riches in his own realm (Dan. 11:38-43).
13. To cause great deceptions (2 Thess. 2:10-12; Jn. 5:43; Dan. 8:25; Rev. 13:1-18).
14. To do according to his own will (Dan. 11:36).
15. To control religion and worship (Dan 11:36; 2 Thess. 2:4; Rev. 13:1-18; 14:9-11; 16:21).
16. To control the lives of all men in his realm (Rev. 13:12-18).
17. To control kings as he wills (Rev. 17:12-17).

18. To make all the other nations fear him (Rev. 13:4).
19. To fight against Christ (Rev. 19:11-21; Dan. 8:25).
20. To reign forty–two months (Rev. 13:5).

His Person

The Antichrist will be a real person and not a religious system or the successive head of a religious system, such as the pope. He is yet to come to power in the future and will literally fulfill all the prophecies concerning himself. His character and characteristics are clearly implied in the points above, which reveal that he will be a man who will possess the talent and leadership qualities found in all gifted conquerors and leaders. In addition to these natural gifts, he will possess the miraculous power of attracting people of every class, fascinating them with his marvelous personality, successes, wisdom, administrative and executive ability, bringing them under his control through his well-directed flattery and masterly diplomacy.

He will be indued with the power of Satan in the exercise of these gifts until the world will wonder after him and many will worship him as God.

Chapter Two

THE TITLES OF THE ANTICHRIST

Antichrist. This is the most common one we use in speaking of him, for he is to be the great opponent of Christ at the end of the age. The word occurs only four times in the Bible (1 Jn. 2:18, 22; 4:3; 2 Jn. 7), but the studies above and below show him to be the one who has claim to that title more than any other, and is to be the one expressly stated to come according to these passages.

The Assyrian (Isa. 10:20-27; 30:18-33; 31:4–32:20; Mic. 5:3-15). The prophecies in these passages were recorded against the Assyrian king in the days of the prophets, but a study of them reveals that they have a latter–day fulfillment in the future Assyrian king who is to oppress Israel just preceding her final restoration. (The Assyrian territory will be part of Antichrist's kingdom and in that sense he is the king of Assyria).

This first passage (Isa. 10:20-27) refers to the "remnant" of Rev. 12:17: "*In that day* the remnant of Israel . . . shall *no more* again stay [Hebrew, look for support] upon him [Antichrist] that smote them; but shall stay upon the Lord . . . O my people *that dwellest in Zion*, be not afraid of *the Assyrian*: he shall smite thee with a rod . . . yet a little while [1,260 days, Rev. 12:6, 14-17; 13:5], and the indignation [Hebrew, God's anger and wrath, the day of vengeance in the Tribulation, as in Isa. 26:20; Dan. 8: 19; 11:36] shall cease, and *mine anger in their destruction . . . in that day* his burden shall be taken away from off thy shoulder . . . the yoke shall be destroyed *because of the anointing*." The Hebrew root for "anointing" is *shawman*, to shine, and no doubt refers to the brightness of Christ's coming in 2 Thess. 2:8-9.

The prophecies in these passages were recorded against the Assyrian king in the days of the prophets, but a study of them reveals that they have a latter–day fulfillment in the future Assyrian king who is to oppress Israel just preceding her final restoration.

The second passage (Isa. 30:18-33) clearly refers to Israel's final restoration under the Messiah: "Therefore will he [the Lord] be exalted . . . the people shall dwell in Zion at Jerusalem: thou shalt weep *no more . . . in the day* that the Lord bindeth the breach of his people . . . the name of the Lord cometh from far, burning with his anger . . . to sift the nations . . . with the flame of a burning fire, with scattering, and tempest, and hailstones. For through the voice of the Lord shall *the Assyrian be beaten down*." (See also Ezek. 38:17-21; 2 Thess. 1:7-10; 2:8-12).

The third passage (Isa. 31:4–32:20) speaks of the same truth: "Like as the lion roaring on his prey . . . shall the Lord of hosts *come down to fight for mount Zion* . . . As birds flying so will the Lord of hosts *defend Jerusalem*; defending also *he will deliver it*; and *passing over he will preserve it* . . . For *in that day* every man shall cast away his idols . . . *then* shall *the Assyrian fall with the sword*, not of a mighty man [but by Christ, 2 Thess. 2:8-9]. . . a king shall reign in righteousness . . . And my people shall dwell in a peaceable

40

habitation, and in sure dwellings, and in quiet resting places."

The last passage (Mic. 5:3-15) definitely speaks of Israel being given up "*Until* the time that she which travaileth hath brought forth [until Israel has brought forth the man-child]: *Then* the remnant of his brethren shall return unto the children of Israel. And he Christ, verses 1 and 21, shall stand and feed in the strength of the Lord . . . now shall he be great *unto the ends of the earth*. And *this man* shall be the peace, *when the Assryian* [Antichrist] *shall come into our land*: and *shall tread in our palaces* . . . thus shall he deliver us from *the Assyrian* . . . I will execute vengeance in anger and fury upon the heathen, such as they have not heard." (See also Dan. 9:27; 11:40-45; 2 Thess. 2: 3-4; Rev. 13).

The king of Babylon (Isa. 14:4). This passage is in a prophecy of Babylon which had a partial fulfillment in the overthrow of Babylon by the Medes and Persians (Isa. 13: 17). The complete fulfillment will be in the last days under the Antichrist, as is proved by the mention of "the day of the Lord" and the restoration of Israel, which will occur when Christ comes to earth in the days of the reign of the Antichrist (Isa. 13:6-16, 19-22; 14:1-8, 18-27). All these prophecies have never been fulfilled as stated here. The Antichrist will be the king of Babylon because he will be the king of Assyria, which will include Babylon.

The spoiler and *the extortioner* (Isa. 16: 1-5). That these terms refer to Antichrist is clear from a study of this passage.

Gog, the chief prince of Meshech and Tubal (Ezek. 38–39). These two chapters will be fulfilled at Armageddon.

The little horn (Dan. 7:8, 24; 8:9, 23).

A king of fierce countenance (Dan. 8: 23).

The prince that shall come (Dan. 9:26, 27). This title refers to the same man as does the "little horn" coming from the ten kingdoms of Revised Rome who will make the seven years covenant with Israel and then break it in the middle of the Week and cause the "abomination of desolation" in the Jewish temple at Jerusalem.

The king of the north (Dan. 11:36-45). This is the king of the Syrian division of the old Grecian Empire as we have seen in our study of Daniel. He is called the "king of the north" because he will come from the division of old Grecian Empire that is north of Palestine. Many Bible scholars say the Antichrist will come from Russia and use this term to prove it, but if "the king of the north" refers to Russia, then what countries are there north of Russia that could fight against Russia, as is required in Dan. 11:44? There are none, so this title applies to the future king of Syria—the northern division of the four divisions of the old Grecian Empire out of which Antichrist must come (Dan. 8:8-9, 20-25).

The man of sin (2 Thess. 2:1-12).

The son of perdition (2 Thess. 2:1-12).

The beast (Dan. 7:11; Rev. 13:1-18; 14:9-11; 15:2-3; 16:2, 10; 17:1-18; 19:19-21; 20: 2-4, 10).

The wicked and ***that wicked*** (Isa. 11:4; 2 Thess. 2:1-12). These last four titles picture the Antichrist in his role as the most sinful and wicked man of his time and perhaps of all time, for he will literally murder multitudes who will not conform to his every desire (Rev. 7:9-17; 13:16-18; 15:1-3; 20: 4-6). For this wickedness he is "the son of perdition," because he is destined to perdition, or destruction and eternal Hell.

Chapter Three

THE "MYSTERY OF INIQUITY"

For the mystery of iniquity doth already work: only he who now letteth will let, until he be taken out of the way (2 Thess. 2:7)

There is a theory that the Antichrist is the "mystery of iniquity" or Satan manifest in the flesh, just as Jesus was the "mystery of godliness," or God manifest in the flesh. This theory futher states that the Antichrist will be "the son of perdition" or the son of Satan by a woman, as Jesus was "the Son of God" by a woman—that the Antichrist is the opposite of Christ in every detail. This theory is false, and can't be supported by Scripture. That the Antichrist is a mysterious personage

These last four titles picture the Antichrist in his role as the most sinful and wicked man of his time and perhaps of all time, for he will literally murder multitudes who will not conform to his every desire.

and will be such a man of mystery in all that he does is false. No statement in Scripture about him is mysterious, or teaches that he will be supernatural, an immortal man from the Abyss, an incarnation of the devil, or a natural son of the devil.

The phrase *mystery of iniquity* literally means "the invisible spirit of lawlessness" or "the evil spirit forces that cause man to sin" (Jn. 8:44; 14:30; Eph. 2:1-3; 1 Jn. 3:8; Eph. 6: 10-18; 2 Cor. 4:3, 4). The same scholars who insist that the Antichrist is the "mystery of iniquity" also teach that he is the beast now bound in the Abyss and will come out again as the Antichrist. They teach that this spirit is Judas who will be reincarnated, and their main argument is that Judas and Antichrist are both called "the son of perdition" (Jn. 17:12; 2 Thess. 2:14). However, no human being has ever gone into the Abyss, nor will one ever go there. Therefore, Judas could not be in the pit in order to come out of it. The expression "the son of perdition" liter-ally means "the son of destruction," because both Judas and the Antichrist are destined to destruction, not because they are natural sons of Satan. They could not be sons of Satan and be the sons of their earthly fathers at the same time. They could not be natural sons of Satan and incarnations of him too, as taught by some.

In the Greek it reads "the son of the destruction" just as it reads "the man of the sin." This last phrase does not limit the Antichrist to being the only "man of sin" and the former phrase does not limit him to be the only "son of destruction." The Hebrews and Greeks called any man who was subject to a particular evil or characteristic, the "son" of that trait, as "sons of Belial" (1 Sam. 1:16; 2:12; 25:17, 25; 1 Ki. 21:10), "child of the devil" (Acts 13:10), "children of the wicked one" (Mt. 13:38), "children of the devil" (1 Jn. 3:10), "children of wisdom" (Lk. 7:35); "children of the world" (Lk. 16:8), "children of light" (Lk. 16:8; Jn. 12:36), "children of disobedience" (Eph. 2:1-3; 5:6-8; Col. 3:6). Also, anyone who was destined to some particular fate was called the "child" of that destiny, as "children of the kingdom" (Mt. 8:12), "children of wrath" (Eph. 2:1-3), "children of the resurrection" (Lk. 20:36). Therefore, in view of this usual practice, it would be only natural to call both Judas and Antichrist "the son of perdition" or destruction, for both are destined to destruction in Hell, because of their sin.

The word "perdition" is used only eight times and is taken from the Greek *apoleia*, meaning "ruin," "loss," "destruction," "perdition," and "perish." It is never used as a name of the devil; hence to call Judas and the Antichrist "sons of the devil" by a woman is not biblical. Neither is it stated in Scripture that Judas ever was, or ever will be, nor that the future Antichrist will be a direct and literal child of the devil by a woman. Try to substitute the word "devil" for "perdition" in all the places in which it is found, and see if it makes sense (Phil. 1:28; 1 Tim. 6:9; Heb. 10:39; 2 Pet. 3:7; Rev. 17:8, 11). The Greek word *apoleia* is translated "destruction" (Mt. 7:13; Rom. 9:22; Phil. 3:19; 2 Pet. 2:1; 3:16), "damnation" (2 Pet. 2:3), "die" (Acts 25:16), "perish" (Acts 8:20), and in other ways, but never as "devil." We can conclude then that "son of perdition" does not mean "son of the devil."

Other statements concerning the Antichrist coming in his own name (Jn. 5:43), exalting himself (2 Thess. 2:4), being worshipped (Rev. 13:8), being cast into Hell (Rev. 19:20), doing his own will (Dan. 11:36), destroying men (Dan. 8:24), and being wicked (2 Thess. 2:3-8), can be understood in connection with any natural, mortal man. If the Antichrist is the "mystery of lawlessness," then he has been here all the time and cannot come from the pit, for Paul said this "mystery" was already working in his day (2 Thess. 2:7). Bible scholars try to find hidden meanings in the Bible—spending a lifetime trying to make the Bible a mystery instead of seeking to make it the simple book it really is. All such hidden interpretations must be rejected for the sake of simple truth.

The devil is never going to have a natural son by a woman. Though some argue that Genesis 3:15 teaches this, it is an improper

49

interpretation of the passage. The seed of the serpent should be understood as the natural offspring of snakes and to the spiritual children of the devil (Mt. 13:38; 1 Jn. 3:8-10; Jn. 8:44). This last passage is taken by some to mean the Antichrist will be a natural seed of the devil, "Ye are of your father the devil . . . When he speaketh a *lie*, he speaketh of his own; for he is a *liar*, and the father of *it*." It is claimed that the word "it" refers to one particular son of the devil, the Antichrist, but this is not only proved false by the same passage that speaks of all men as being "of your father the devil," but it is also proved ridiculous by same passage. The "lie" refers to a literal lie and not to a natural son of the devil by a woman. If the "lie" here means the natural son of the devil that he is going to have by a woman, then he is going to "speak" this son into existence. If this be true, then he could not be a natural son by a woman or by an incarnation of himself, as some teach.

It is also argued that Judas was the only one ever called a "devil," thus proving further that he was the devil incarnate, or that he was the "mystery of iniquity," and a "son of perdition" (Jn. 6:70-71; 17:12). The definite article is used, thus making Judas "the devil," but the definite article is not in the Greek at all, which means "a devil." The Greek word for devil is *diabolos* and means "adversary" or "slanderer" and is used of other men who are called "false accusers" (2 Tim. 3:3; Titus 2:3) and "slanderers" (1 Tim. 3:11). The word never implies an incarnation, as some argue. If so, then these other men who are slanderers (devils) were also incarnations of the devil, and in this case the above theory is destroyed. The devil never incarnates himself in the Antichrist any more than he did Judas, for the Dragon is always seen as a separate person outside the Beast.

If the Antichrist is going to be the devil incarnate, then we would have to conclude that the devil has not yet come (1 Jn. 2:18; Jn. 5:43), that he will not come until after ten kingdoms are formed inside the Roman Empire (Dan. 7:24) and after the rapture of the Church (2 Thess. 2:7-8), that he will continue only forty–two months when he does

51

come (Rev. 13:5), that the devil is a "man" (Rev. 13:18), that this man is in Heaven now accusing the saints and will be cast out of Heaven in the middle of the Week (Rev. 12:7-17; 13:1-8), that the Dragon is not a separate person outside the Beast as he is pictured as being in all passages on the subject (Rev. 13: 2-4; 16:13-16; 19:20; 20:10), that the devil is to be "slain" by Christ at His Second Advent (Dan. 7:11; Isa. 11:4; 2 Thess. 2:8-9), that he is to be put into two different places during the Millennium, for the Beast is in the Lake of Fire and the Dragon is in the Abyss during that time (Rev. 19:20; 20:1-3), that the devil is still in the Lake of Fire while he is loosed at the end of the Millennium and that he will be again cast back where he already is and has always been since Armageddon (Rev. 19:20; 20:1-10), and that the devil has died once and will die twice in the future if we are to believe the theories of men concerning Antichrist.

Chapter Four

THE FALSE PROPHET

The Beast Out of the Earth

And I beheld another beast coming up out of the earth; and he had two horns like a lamb, and he spake as a dragon. And he exerciseth all the power of the first beast before him, and causeth the earth and them which dwell therein to worship the first beast, whose deadly wound was healed. And he doeth great wonders, so that he maketh fire come down from heaven on the earth in the sight of men, And deceiveth them that dwell on the earth by the means of those miracles which he had power to do in the sight of the beast; saying to them that dwell on the earth, that they should make an image to the

53

beast, which had the wound by a sword, and did live. And he had power to give life unto the image of the beast, that the image of the beast should both speak, and cause that as many as would not worship the image of the beast should be killed. And he causeth all, both small and great, rich and poor, free and bond, to receive a mark in their right hand, or in their foreheads: And that no man might buy or sell, save he that had the mark, or the name of the beast, or the number of his name (Rev. 13:11-17)

The "second beast," is mentioned in this passage for the first time, and all that we know about him in the Bible is recorded in the book of Revelation. He is called "the false prophet" (Greek, *pseudoprophetes*) in Rev. 16:13; 19:20; 20:10, which are the only other passages that mention him. He is to be a prophet, but a false one; a prophet of the Antichrist, not of Christ. In Revelation 16:13 he is seen with the Beast and Dragon sending forth the demon spirits to gather the nations to Armageddon. In Revelation 19:20 he is seen as being the miracle–working co–laborer and leader of the nations along with the first beast as he comes against Christ at Armageddon. The doom of this second beast will be torment in the Lake of Fire forever along with the first beast, the dragon, and all rebellious creatures (Rev. 20:10). The facts concerning him and his ministry in Revelation 13:11-17 are:

1.   He is seen coming on the scene of action by John after the vision of the first beast (Rev. 13:11). He is called "another" beast, from Greek *altos*, meaning "another of the same kind," "denoting numerical distinction;" "the second of two where there may be more," as in Matthew 10:23 and John 18:15. Therefore, this beast is the second one in this chapter and cannot possibly be the same as the first beast of Revelation 13:1-10. If there were only one beast, there would not be two descriptions and statements concerning two different beasts. This point is so clear in this passage that we need not take up the many points of contrast between the two beasts.

2.   This beast is seen coming up "out of the earth" (Rev. 13:11). The word "earth" is the same as "world" in Rev. 13:3 and "earth" in Rev. 13:12. Here it symbolizes the peoples on the earth, as in Dan. 7:1-7, 17. The word "sea" is also used in a symbolical sense of peoples in Revelation 13:1-8; 17:1, 15 and Daniel 7:1-7, 17. The phrase "out of the earth" is the same in meaning as "out of the sea," as is proved by a similar construction in Daniel 7:3 and 17 where four beasts came up "out of the sea" and in the interpretation they are said to be four kingdoms coming up out of the earth. This does not mean that this beast comes out of the underworld of spirits and is a resurrected or reincarnated man that has lived on the earth before, as is taught by some. It does not mean this any more than it does when four kingdoms are spoken of as coming out of the earth in Daniel 7:17.

Some teach that this beast is Judas who will come up out of the underworld, because his characteristics are like those of Judas. Arguments based upon similar acts in the lives of these men are not sufficient proof of this theory. Others claim that the first beast will be Judas from the underworld, but, as we have seen, no human being can come up from the underworld and fulfill the office of either of these beasts. The beasts symbolize two natural men, as the sea and earth symbolize peoples. They are yet of the future and will be born and live natural lives like all other men. They will rise in power out of the peoples of the earth to carry out their intended missions of these prophecies in the will of God.

3. The second beast has two horns making him look like a lamb but he speaks as a dragon. His lamb–like appearance will make him a fit man for his office, thus causing him to be looked upon as a wonderful prophet and man of religion. Combined with this lamb–like appearance will be his dragon or serpent–like deceiving speech. This, and a few miracles, will complete his method of deception. The expression "spake as a dragon" should read "was speaking as a dragon," showing that when John saw him coming out of the mass of humanity, his speech was one of the most conspicuous things about him.

4.   He will exercise all the power of the first beast before him and cause the earth to worship the first beast, whose deadly wound will be healed" (Rev. 13:12). He will be the executive of Antichrist and exercise Satan's power, which will be given to the first beast (Rev. 13:2-4; 2 Thess. 2:8-12). The length of the existence of this second beast in power is not stated, but he is not to rise until after the first one does, so it cannot be for more than 3½ years. He will exercise this power before or in the presence of the Antichrist. He is never mentioned apart from the Antichrist, so it must be that the two will work in close union and will withstand the two witnesses as Jannes and Jambres withstood Moses in power and miracles (2 Tim. 3:8).

5.   "He doeth great wonders, so that he maketh fire to come down from Heaven on the Earth in the sight of men" (Rev. 13:13). The purpose of these signs wrought by the False Prophet is to deceive men to accept the Antichrist as God. He "deceiveth them that dwell on the earth by the means of those miracles which he had power to do in the sight

of the beast" (Rev 13:14). Satan has continually deceived the whole world (Rev. 12:9), but here he has planned the worst deception ever known, which is to be permitted of God, because men receive not the love of the truth that they might be saved (2 Thess. 2:8-12; Rev. 9:20-21; 13:3, 12-18; 14:9; 16:2; 1 Tim. 4:1-3). He will deceive and use these signs to further impress his deception, for miracles alone are no complete and definite proof of a divine mission. Just as the Lord's signs were for the purpose of impressing the people and causing them to believe in Him, so these also will be to impress those who may not be ready to believe in the Beast.

> *Satan has continually deceived the whole world (Rev. 12:9), but here he has planned the worst deception ever known, which is to be permitted of God, because men receive not the love of the truth that they might be saved.*

6.   The "beast out of the earth" will tell those dwelling on the earth to make an image to the first beast. The image will be made and set up in the temple of God to be worshipped (Mt. 24:15). He will have the power to give

life to this image that it should both speak and cause all who will not worship it to be killed. This will be a wonderful sign in itself, that a material image should be given power to speak and act (Rev. 13:14-15).

7. The second beast will cause all classes to receive brands in their right hands or in their foreheads, that no man might buy or sell except those who have them (Rev. 13: 16-18). This will result in the martyrdom of most of the "great multitude, which no man could number, of all nations" (Rev. 7:9-17; 13:7; 14:13; 15:2-3; 20:4). In the worship of the first beast and his image, men will be so devoted as to say, "Who is like unto the beast? Who is able to make war with him?" This reveals the worship will be both political and religious (Rev. 13:4). It will not be a willing worship on the part of many, for force will be used to make them worship. The worship will be of such an apostate nature as to pronounce eternal doom to all who partake (Rev. 14:9-11). Many men will throw overboard all faith in God and Christ, become servants of the devil, and be con-

trolled by demon spirits to such an extent as to be past redemption.

The three brands that followers of Antichrist may choose are:

1. "A mark," or in the Greek, "the mark." That this mark is different from either the name, or the number of his name, is clear from the following passages where the three brands are enumerated (Rev. 13:16-18; 14:9; 15:2-4; 20:4). What kind of mark it will be is not revealed, but it will be a literal mark in the flesh (Rev. 13:16; 14:9). Perhaps it will be the emblem of the kingdom of the Antichrist.

2. "The name of the beast"; that is, of the first beast (Rev. 13:17).

3. "The number of his name" (Rev. 13: 17-18; 15:2). The idea is that the letters in the name of the Antichrist will equal 666. In the Hebrew and Greek languages there is no separate system of numbers as in the English. The letters of the alphabet also stand for numbers, so the numerical value of the

letters in the name of the future Antichrist (whatever they will be) will equal 666. This will be "the number of a man" (Rev. 13:18). There are many Greek and Hebrew names that have a numerical value of 666 (just like any number of combinations of English numbers equals 666). There is no hidden meaning to the number, for the very expression "Here is wisdom" (native insight, understanding) shows that it is easy to understand.

The brands of the beast cannot be taken until the last 3½ years of this age, or during the Great Tribulation. Therefore, it is impossible for one to take any of his brands, or worship him today, for he is not now on the scene. When he does come and these things begin to be fulfilled those who take any one of the brands, or worship him, will be doomed to eternal Hell, and in this life will be plagued by the vial plagues (Rev. 14:9-11; 16:1-21). No one will ever know what the mark, or the name of the Beast will be until after he comes, which will be after the rapture and after the ten kingdoms are formed inside the old Roman Empire territory, as we have already seen. Although we cannot know what the Antichrist's mark or name will be, we can know what the numerical value of his name is, for it is already revealed as being 666 (Rev. 13:18). This, and this alone, is all that we will ever get to know of the three brands until Antichrist comes and fulfills Revelation 13. When he comes all men will know what his name will be, and they can then see what combination of letters he will have in his name that equals 666.

A study of the Antichrist is not complete without a look at the Great Tribulation, which will be caused by the actions of the Antichrist himself. His actions and their consequences will be studied in the next chapter.

Chapter Five

THE TRIBULATION

The Time and Length of the Tribulation

Tribulation will begin to affect Israel before the Seventieth Week of Daniel 9 begins; how long before is not certain, but when Antichrist rises at the beginning of the Week, Israel will be undergoing persecution by the harlot and the ten kings of Revised Rome who are dominated by the harlot until the middle of the Week. The Antichrist will come out of one of the ten kingdoms mentioned in the first chapter, and he will make a seven–year covenant with Israel, assuring them of protection in their continued establishment

> *Tribulation will begin to affect Israel before the Seventieth Week of Daniel 9 begins; when Antichrist rises at the beginning of the Week, Israel will be undergoing persecution by the harlot and the ten kings of Revised Rome who are dominated by the harlot until the middle of the Week.*

as a nation (Dan. 9:27). There will be a wide-spread persecution of the Jews and "they shall be hated of all nations" during the time of "the beginning of sorrows" when Antichrist will be endeavoring to conquer all these nations (Mt. 24:4-12). The Antichrist will need Jewish support to help him rise over these nations, so he will make an alliance with them for seven years. Therefore, tribulation will occur during the whole of Daniel's Seventieth Week (Dan. 9:27). It will end at the Second Coming of Christ (Mt. 24:29-31).

The Divisions of the Tribulation

THE FIRST DIVISION takes in the first 3½ years of the Seventieth Week of Daniel 9 and is termed "the lesser tribulation," for it is not as great in severity as the last 3½ years, because of the protection of Israel by the Antichrist during that time. Israel's per-secution in the first 3½ years will be from a source entirely different from that of the last division. In these latter years she will be persecuted by the harlot and the ten kings.

This division of the Tribulation takes in the fulfillment of Revelation 6:1–9:21. The judgments of the sixth seal and first six trumpets comes in this period, thus proving tribulation during this time.

THE LAST DIVISION takes in the last 3½ years of the Week and is termed "the Great Tribulation" because it will be more severe in persecution upon Israel than the first 3½ years. The Antichrist, who will protect Israel the first 3½ years, will break his covenant with her in the middle of the Week and become her most bitter enemy. He will then try to destroy her, which calls for the judgments of the seven vials of the last 3½ years. This part of the Tribulation includes the fulfillment of Revelation 10:1–19: 21. Jesus, Daniel, Jeremiah, and many others speak of this time of Israel's trouble as being worse than any time that has ever been on earth or ever will be (Dan. 12:1; Jer. 30:4-11; Mt. 24: 21-22; Rev. 11:1-2; 12:14-17; 13:5-7).

> *The Antichrist, who will protect Israel the first 3½ years, will break his covenant with her in the middle of the Week and become her most bitter enemy.*

The Purpose of the Tribulation

1. To purify Israel and bring them back to a place where God can fulfill the everlasting covenants made with their fathers (Isa. 2:6; 3:26; 16:1-5; 24:1-25; 26:20-21; Ezek. 20:33-34; 22:17-22; Rom. 11:25-29).
2. To purify Israel of all rebels (Ezek. 20: 33-34; 22:17-22; Zech. 13:8-9; Mal. 3: 3-4).
3. To plead with and bring Israel into the bond of the New Covenant (Ezek. 20: 33-34; 36:24-28; Jer. 30:3-11; Zech. 12: 10–13:9; Mal. 4:3-4).
4. To judge Israel and punish them for their rejection of the Messiah and make them willing to accept Him when He comes the second time (Ezek. 20:33-34; Zech. 12:10–13:9; 14:1-15; Mt. 24: 15-31).
5. To judge the nations for their persecution of Israel (Isa. 63:1-5; Joel 3; Rev. 6:1–19:21).
6. To bring Israel to complete repentance

(Zech. 12:10–13:9; Rom. 11:26-29; Mt. 23:39).

7. To fulfill the prophecies of Dan. 9:24-27; Rev. 6:1–19:21; Mt. 24:15, 29.

8. To cause Israel to flee into the wilderness of Edom and Moab and to be so persecuted by the nations that Israel will have to turn to God for help (Isa. 16:1-5; Ezek. 20:33-35; Dan. 11:40–12:7; Hos. 2:14-17; Mt. 24:15-31; Rev. 12).

The Character of the Tribulation

The character of the tribulation can easily be understood in view of God's wrath being poured out upon mankind for their wickedness and corruption, which will exceed the days of Noah and Lot (Gen. 6; Mt. 24:37-39; Lk. 17:22-37; 2 Tim. 3:1-12). Men will reject the truth until God turns them over to the "strong delusion" of the Antichrist who will cause them to believe a lie and be damned (2 Thess. 2:8-12; 2 Pet. 3:1-9). Even after God pours out His judgments upon men, they will still defy Him (Rev. 9:20-21; 6:2-11; 17:1-18; 18:1-24). Words cannot describe the utter rebellion and wickedness of men during this period of final struggle between God and the devil over possession of the earth (Rev. 11:15; 12:7-12; 19:11-21; 20:1-3).

Will the Tribulation Be Worldwide?

The old theory that the Tribulation will be worldwide is not stated in even one scripture. On the contrary, the Bible is clear that the Antichrist will not reign over the whole world, but only over the ten kingdoms that are to be formed inside the old Roman Empire territory. Most of the judgments of the trumpets and vials are stated as being only upon a third or fourth part of the earth (Rev. 8:7-12), and upon "the men which had the mark of the beast" and "upon the seat [throne] of the beast: and his kingdom" (Rev. 16:2, 10, 12). However, nothing is said as to the limitation of the extent of the demon–locusts or of the extent of the devil's wrath when he is cast out (Rev. 9:1-11; 12:7-12). The sixth trumpet kills only a third part of men (Rev. 9:12-21).

When we speak of "the tribulation" we mean the troubles that God's people will have to undergo, especially the Jewish people, as Daniel's Seventieth Week concerns only Israel and their city Jerusalem. The last half of the Week will be "the time of Jacob's trouble" and these troubles primarily concern Israel. The Tribulation will not be worldwide, even if it covers all lands that Christians live in after the rapture. Unknown tribes of people in the interior of many lands will not know of the tribulation caused by the Antichrist.

Appendix One

BIBLICAL STUDIES

I. THE BIBLE IS EASY TO UNDERSTAND

We've reached the end of our study of the Antichrist, but we're not finished yet! God's Word presents us with a lifetime of study opportunities, but where are we supposed to start? This chapter is designed to give you the tools you'll need to study the Bible for yourself. The Bible is a simple book to understand. We've seen that as we've studied a topic that many consider complex and obscure. Even biblical prophecy, an area of Scripture that many assume to be beyond comprehension, is as easy to understand as the accounts of Jonah, Daniel or Joseph. This probably sounds ridiculous to most people, but perhaps considering a few simple facts will change your mind! Consider the following points:

The Bible is a Revelation. The Bible is an inspired revelation from God. A revelation is an uncovering or unveiling so that everyone may see what was previously covered or hidden.

The Bible Contains Many Repeated Truths. Over and over the Bible repeats truth so that "in the mouth of two or three witnesses every word may be established" (Dt. 17:6-7; 19:15; Mt. 18:16; 2 Cor. 13:1; 1 Tim. 5:19; Heb. 10:28). Because of this fact, any doctrine that is not plainly stated in Scripture is best left alone. When God says something about a particular topic, it will be found repeated in several places, so we will not be left in doubt

> *When God says something about a particular topic, it will be found repeated in several places, so we will not be left in doubt as to what God says.*

as to what God says. Our part is to collect everything God says on a subject—making it so clear that no interpretation is necessary. If we do this, nothing will need to be added to or taken from the Bible in order to understand the truth. All we need to do is to find out where "it is written" and then believe it.

72

We must always make our ideas conform to the Bible and not the Scripture to our ideas.

The Bible is Written in Simple Language. It is intended to be read and understood without interpretation. All God considers necessary to understand the Bible is childlike faith. God made both man and His Word, and they fit together as a lock and key (Job 32:8; 38:3-6; Jn. 1:4-9). Even the ungodly can understand if they so desire (Rom. 1:16-20).

The Bible is a Simple Book to Understand Because Most of it is Either History or Simple Instructions About How to Live. About 25,007 verses of the Bible—about 80 percent of it—contain simple history, commands, warnings, promises, rebukes, and plain instructions by means of which men may understand the will of God. The remaining 20 percent (or 6,207 verses) are prophecy written in the same simple human language that is used to record history. Of these 6,207 prophetic verses, 3,299 have been fulfilled and are now history. The 2,908 other verses are unfulfilled prophecy.

II. THE TRUE METHOD OF BIBLE INTERPRETATION

The fundamental principle is to gather from the Scriptures themselves the precise meaning the writers intended to convey. It applies to the Bible the same principles, rules, grammatical process, and exercise of common sense and reason that we apply to other books. In doing this, one must understand the Bible literally when it is at all possible. When a statement is found that cannot possibly be literal, as Jesus being a "door" or of a woman being clothed with the sun and standing on the moon and on her head a crown of twelve stars, or of land animals coming out of the sea, and other statements which are obviously not literal, then we know the language is figurative. In such cases we must get the literal truth conveyed by the figurative language, and the truth intended to be conveyed will be as literal as if it were expressed in literal language without the use of such figures. After all, figurative language expresses literal truth as much as if such figures were not used. In a general sense, the true method of Bible interpretation embraces the following ideas:

1. The primary meaning of words and their common use in a particular age in which they are used, and the importance of synonyms.
2. The grammatical construction and idiomatic peculiarities of the languages of the Bible, and the meaning of the context, both immediate and remote.
3. Comparison of parallel passages on the same subject.
4. The purpose or object of each writer in each particular book.
5. The historical background of each writer and the circumstances under which he wrote.
6. The general plan of the entire Bible, and its moral and spiritual teachings.
7. The agreement of Scripture in its several parts, and its prophecies and their fulfillment.
8. The manners and customs of the particular age and land of each writer.

9. Understanding of how to interpret prophecy, poetry, allegories, symbols, parables, figures of speech, types and all other forms of human expression.

When all these facts are kept in mind and all scriptures interpreted in harmony with all these principles, there cannot possibly be any misunderstanding of any part of the Bible.

IV. GENERAL RULES OF BIBLE INTERPRETATION

1. The entire Bible came from God and possesses unity of design and teaching. We shall, therefore, consider both Testaments together as being equally inspired.

2. It may be assumed that no one resorts to speech or writing without having some idea to express; that in order to express that idea he will use words and forms of speech familiar to his hearers or readers; and that if he uses a word or figure of speech in a different sense from what is commonly understood he will make the fact known.

3. The Bible cannot contradict itself. Its teachings in one part must agree with its teachings in another part. Therefore, any interpretation which makes the Bible inconsistent with itself must rest upon false principles.

4. No meaning should be gotten from the Bible except that which a fair and honest, grammatical, and historical interpretation yields.

5. Language is an accumulation of words used to interchange thoughts. To understand the language of the speaker or writer, it is necessary to know the meaning of his words. A true meaning of the words is a true meaning of the sense. It is as true of the Bible as of any other book.

6. Often to fully understand a passage of Scripture, the scope or plan of the entire book must be known. Sometimes the design of the books are made clear, as in the case of Proverbs (1:1-4); Isaiah (1:1-3); John (20:31); Revelation (1:1); etc. If the definite purpose of the book is not stated, the purpose of

the book must be gotten from the contents and from the design of the Bible as a whole, as is clear in Jn. 5:39; 2 Tim. 2:15; 3:16-17. Some seeming contradictions are cleared up when this rule is observed. The difference between Paul and James is easily understood when the design of their books is understood and recognized. In Romans, Paul seeks to prove that a man is not saved by works, while in James he seeks to show that a man cannot remain saved unless he brings forth good works.

7. Sometimes the connection is obscured through the use of virtual dialogue between the writers and unseen persons, as in Ps. 15; Isa. 52:13; 63:1-6; Rom. 3; etc.

8. One of the most fundamental rules of interpretation is that of comparing Scripture with Scripture. It is by a strict and honest observance of this rule that the true meaning can be gotten when every other thing has failed to make clear the meaning. Before arriving at the whole truth, be sure that all the scriptures on a subject are collected together

and read at one time. If there is any question left after you have done this, then go over the whole subject carefully until every question is cleared up.

10.   In some places a statement on a subject may be very brief and seemingly obscure and will be made perfectly clear by a larger passage on the same subject. Always explain the seemingly difficult with the more simple scriptures. No doctrine founded upon a single verse of Scripture contains the whole of the subject; so do not be dishonest and wrest with Scripture or force a meaning into a passage that is not clearly understood in the passage or in parallel passages on the same subject.

11.   The progressive character of revelation and the gradual development of truth should be recognized. Some truths found in germ in the Old Testament are fully developed in the New Testament. For example, the idea of blood sacrifices was developed from the time of Abel until it was fully culminated and made eternally clear in the sacrifice of Christ on Calvary.

12. The meaning of a word or phrase in the New Testament must not be carried back into Old Testament doctrine unless such is warranted by both Testaments. For example, water baptism, the Lord's Supper, and other New Testament doctrines are not found in the Old Testament at all. It is not proper to ask whether David was baptized in water, or whether Saul was a Christian, because these are New Testament terms.

13. Passages obviously literal should not be spiritualized. For example, making the natural blessings of Canaan the spiritual blessings of Heaven; regarding the ark of Noah as salvation through Christ, and hundreds of like interpretations.

14. The dispensational character of Scripture should be noted so that one can pigeonhole every passage of Scripture in some definite period in God's plan.

15. The three classes of people (the Jews, the Church, and the Gentiles) dealt with in Scripture should be noted. Up to Genesis 12, the race as a whole is dealt with. From

Gen. 12 to the New Testament the Jews and the Gentiles are dealt with; and in the New Testament these and the Church of God, made up of Jews and Gentiles, are dealt with (1 Cor. 10:32).

16.   In all study of doctrine the practical aspect must be kept in view (2 Tim. 3:16-17).

17.   The comparative importance of truth should be emphasized. The positive truths should be studied more than the negative. It is more important to have faith instead of unbelief; to know God better than Satan, etc. So one should learn more about faith and God than unbelief and Satan.

18.   General familiarity with the Bible as a whole is very important. Keep reading the Bible over and over until its contents as a whole are familiar. The more one can remember here and there what he has read, the clearer the Bible will become.

19.   Words of Scripture must agree with the content and the subject matter in the passages where found. No meaning should be

given to a word that would be in the least out of harmony with any scripture. For example, the word "seen" in John 1:18 should be understood to mean "comprehended" in order to harmonize with all scriptures that state men saw God with the natural eyes.

20. Careful attention should be paid to connecting words that connect events with each other, as the word "when," "then," etc., in Mt. 24:15-16, 21, 23, 40; 25:1.

21. Careful attention should be paid to prepositions, definite articles, names of different persons and places with the same name, same persons and places with different names, and the names of different persons and places that are spelled differently by different authors in different books.

22. Ascertain the exact meaning of the words of Scripture. The way a word is used, the subject matter, and the context often determine the true meaning.

23. Hebrew and Greek idioms should be noted. Sometimes a person having a peculiar

characteristic, or subject to a peculiar evil, or destined to a particular destiny is called the "child" of that evil or destiny (Lk. 10:6; Eph. 2:1-3; 2 Thess. 2:3). The word *father* is applied to the originator of any custom or to the inventor of something (Gen. 4:20-21; Jn. 8:44). It is also used for "ancestor" (1 Chr. 1:17). The words "son" and "daughter" are sometimes used of descendants or in–laws. (Gen. 46:22; Lk. 3:23). The words "brother" and "cousin" are sometimes used of relatives and countrymen (Gen. 14:16 with 11:31; Lk. 1:36, 58). Names of parents are used of posterity (1 Ki. 18:17-18).

24. Preference is sometimes expressed by the word "hate" (Lk. 14:26; Rom. 9:13).

25. A peculiar idiom concerning numbers must be understood. Sometimes round numbers rather than the exact number are used (Judg. 20:35, 46). This will explain seeming contradictions between numbers. Failure to understand this idiom may have caused copyists and translators to misunderstand the numbers of some passages which seem erroneous

and very large. For example, in 1 Samuel 6: 19, we read the Lord smote in a very small town 50,070 people, which, in the Hebrew text reads, "seventy men two fifties and one thousand" or 70–100–1,000, or 1,170 people.

26. Careful attention should be paid to parenthesis, the use of italics (meaning these words are not in the original but supplied in English to make sense), the use of capital letters, marginal notes, references, summaries of chapters, chapter and page headings, the division of the text into chapters and verses, punctuation, obsolete English words, the rendering of the same original words by different English words, and other things about the English translations. All these things are human additions to the original text and should not be relied upon. For example, the running of references to prove a doctrine is sometimes misleading. The references may not be on the same subject, as can be easily detected by the reader.

27. Seeming contradictions in Scripture should be considered in the light of all the

principles stated above. It must be kept in mind that the Bible records sayings of men under pressure of trials who said things that they never would have said otherwise. It records sayings of backsliders and rebels against God. It records statements of Satan and demons, and the words of such rebels should never be taken as the words from the mouth of God. They should not always be held as truth, for sometimes they are lies. Inspiration guarantees that these rebels said those things, but it does not guarantee that what they said is truth. Sometimes such statements contradict those of God and good men under divine utterance. Enemies of God take such contradictions between what God says and what rebels against God say and use them to prove the Bible contradicts itself. Naturally, such contradictions are found in the Bible, but they are not contradictions between statements made by God. The only statements that can be relied upon as truth are those that come from God and men who speak for God as the Spirit gives utterance, and in these there is no contradiction.

The Bible also records the changes of God's will and plan in a later age over that of an earlier one. Such changes have been taken by the ungodly as contradictions, but such have had to be made by God because of the sin and rebellion of the people to whom He promised such things and for whom He made a certain plan. For example, in Gen. 1:31 God saw everything that He had made and it was good, but in Gen. 6:6 God repented that He had made man. In the meantime, between the two passages, sin and rebellion had entered, which made it necessary for God to have a changed attitude toward man. God has had to change his plan temporarily because of man's sin, but the original and eternal plan of God for creation has never been changed and never will be. God will finally realize His original purpose; that is the reason for His present dispensational dealings. God deals with each generation as circumstances demand. Sometimes God has had to change His promises to a certain group because they refused to meet the conditions for the fulfillment of these promises.

28. The seeming contradictions in the New Testament will also vanish and will be cleared up if men would be as fair with God as they will want God to be with them in the judgment. Always look for an explanation and it will be found. For example, men criticize the Bible for lack of harmony between the temptations of Christ in Mt. 4, and those in Lk. 4. But when we consider the fact that there were two separate sets of temptations during the forty days, and that after the first set of tests in Luke, Satan was dismissed "for a season," and after the last set of tests in Matthew, Satan was dismissed for good, there is no contradiction. The seeming contradictions between the sermons of Mt. 5 and Lk. 6 are cleared up when we see that there were two sermons—one on the mount and the other "in the plain." The so–called contradictions of the Bible are unreal and imaginary. Because of the lack of information as to the time, places, circumstances, etc., men cannot always judge concerning them. So it would be best always to give God the benefit of the doubt, since He knows all things and

was there when things happened. If He did not see fit to give all details so as to make every small detail clear, that is His wisdom. It should not detract from faith in God and His revelation.

All seeming contradictions in the Bible are easily cleared up with a better knowledge of the text, by correct translation, by knowing the manners and customs of the age and the country in which the books were written, by a wider application of historical facts, and by a fair and sane application of the rules of interpretation given above.

Appendix Two

KEYS TO UNDERSTANDING THE BOOK OF REVELATION

I. Literalness of the Book

The book of Revelation admittedly contains both literal and figurative language. It is to be understood literally wherever possible. In other words, when a statement is made, it should be taken to mean just what is written unless such interpretation should be highly improbable and contrary to the dictates of rhetoric and spiritually–enlightened reason, or contrary to scriptures elsewhere on the same subject. In view of this test, if the passage does not admit a literal interpretation, then, of course, we must look elsewhere for an explanation. This is the only sound method of interpretation, as is clear from the fact that the book is a revelation in itself. To treat it as a mystery or to spiritualize it is to deny what it professes to be. Every scene and every truth in the book is clearly explained in the book itself. The reader should first discover what the book itself says concerning its own truths and revelations before searching the remainder of the scriptures for additional light upon the subject in question. Pre–revelation prophecy will throw much light upon many passages in Revelation and help in a more detailed study of almost every truth in the book. This revelation is in perfect harmony with all the preceding prophecies and is the logical and harmonious completion of them.

II. The Key to the interpretation

> Write the things which thou hast seen, and the things which are, and the things which shall be hereafter (Rev. 1:19)

There is a natural three–fold division to the book of Revelation, as expressed in the verse cited above. One has only to believe this division, as given by Christ, to understand the book fully, especially as to the time of the fulfillment of the things of each division.

PART I. "The things which thou hast seen"; that is, Christ in the midst of the seven candlesticks (Rev. 1:12-18, 20), as seen by John before he began to write.

2. PART II. "The things which are"; that is, the things concerning the churches then existent and those which should exist throughout the church age to the rapture. This division takes in only Revelation 2–3.

3. PART III. "The things which shall be hereafter"; that is, the things which shall come to pass after the rapture of the Church. This division includes all of the events of Revelation 4–22.

The moment these divisions are forgotten and the reader begins to disarrange them and insert certain things into the one or the other that are not part of the division, he will become confused as to the divine order of these "things" which are so clearly given in consecutive order, and he will miss the true intent of the "things" written therein. That we refrain from confusing these "things" is absolutely imperative if a true understanding of them is to be gained.

To further prove that everything in Revelation 4–22 must occur after the rapture of the Church, we have this fact confirmed in Revelation 4:1. After John had recorded the vision of Christ in Revelation 1, completing the first division of the book, and after he had recorded all that Christ told him to write to the churches in Revelation 2–3, completing the second division of the book, he was told in Revelation 4:1 that he was to see "things which *must be* hereafter," that is, after the events pertaining to the churches of the second division of the book. Therefore, if everything from Revelation 4:1 on through the rest of the book *must be* after the churches, then all the events of Revelation 4–22 must be after the churches. If they *must be* after

After John had recorded the vision of Christ in Revelation 1, completing the first division of the book, and after he had recorded all that Christ told him to write to the churches in Revelation 2–3, completing the second division of the book, he was told in Revelation 4:1 that he was to see "things which must be hereafter," that is, after the events pertaining to the churches of the second division of the book.

the churches, then they cannot happen during the time of the churches. If they cannot happen during the time of the churches, then the Church is no longer on the earth during the fulfillment of the things which *must be* after the churches.

Revelation 4:1 literally reads in the Greek, "*After these things* [the things concerning the churches of the previous division] I saw, and behold a door opened in heaven, and the first voice [of Rev. 1:10] which I heard was as a trumpet speaking with me, saying, Come up hither, and I will show to thee *what things must take place after these things*," that is, *after* the churches of which John wrote in the previous chapters.

These three divisions of Revelation mentioned above do not overlap, nor are they concurrent. One division must be completely fulfilled before the other begins. So if one will be fair and understand that every event of Revelation 4:1 on through the rest of the book *must be* fulfilled after the rapture of the Church, and if he does not bring one of these events back and place it among the churches

as being fulfilled before the rapture, everything in the book will be clearly understood.
Most of the false theories of Revelation have
come into being because interpreters have
failed to recognize the natural threefold division of the book. It is true, most interpreters
emphasize these divisions in the beginning of
their interpretations of the book, but when it
comes to keeping all the events of Revelation
4–22 after the churches they generally fail to
maintain their consistency. They will place
some of the events of the seals, trumpets,
and vials back in the church age and explain
them as being fulfilled before the rapture.
They will explain the "woman" and the
"man child" in connection with the church of
this age, whereas Jesus told John they were
part of the "things" which *must be* after the
churches. They will interpret the Dragon, the
Beast, the False Prophet, or some other event
of Revelation 4–22 as being fulfilled along
with the churches, while the truth is they are
part of the things which *must be* after the
churches. If the reader will watch this he will
have the knowledge to place these events of